PRIMATES

PRIMATES

DAVE BEATY

PHOTO RESEARCH
Charles Rotter/Gary Lopez Productions

PHOTO CREDITS
COMSTOCK/Boyd Norton: front cover, 29
COMSTOCK/George Lepp: back cover
COMSTOCK/Russ Kinne: 2, 9, 11, 15, 25, 31
COMSTOCK/Phyllis Greenberg: 13, 19
David C. Fritts: 17
Kevin Schafer & Martha Hill: 21
Zoological Society of San Diego: 23
Jeanne Drake: 27

Text Copyright © 1993 by The Child's World, Inc.
All rights reserved. No part of this book may be
reproduced or utilized in any form or by any means
without written permission from the Publisher.
Printed in the United States of America.

Distributed to schools and libraries in the United States by
ENCYCLOPAEDIA BRITANNICA EDUCATIONAL CORP.
310 South Michigan Avenue
Chicago, Illinois 60604

Library of Congress Cataloging-in-Publication Data
Beaty, Dave, 1965-
Primates / by Dave Beaty.
p. cm.
Summary: Introduces the physical characteristics and
behavior of various primates, including the mountain
gorilla, bush baby, and mandrill.
ISBN 0-89565-851-8

1. Primates--Juvenile literature.	[1. Primates.]	I. Title.
QL737.P9B37 1993		92-3082
599.8--dc20		CIP
		AC

CONTENTS

Introduction 6

Bush Babies 8

Ring-tailed Lemurs 10

Ruffed Lemurs 12

Cotton-top Marmosets 14

Japanese Macaques 16

Siamang Monkeys 18

Spider Monkeys 20

Red Uakaris 22

Mandrills 24

Chimpanzees 26

Mountain Gorillas 28

Orangutans 30

Of all the animals in the world, perhaps none spark as much interest as primates. Monkeys, apes, and prosimians are all primates. Humans are primates, too. Almost all primates live in groups of some sort. They are also among the most intelligent animals on earth.

Prosimians are the least humanlike of the primates. They include tree shrews, lemurs, bush babies, lorises, and tarsiers. Most prosimians sleep during the day and are active at night. Prosimians live in warm, tropical forests of Africa, Asia, and South America.

There are about 200 different kinds of monkeys. They live in the same tropical forests as prosimians. Like other primates, monkeys are agile climbers and leapers. They spend most of their time in the trees and rarely venture to the ground.

There are four types of apes—chimpanzees, orangutans, gorillas, and gibbons. Apes live in Asia and Africa. They all are larger and smarter than monkeys. Because of their size, apes usually stay on the ground. Some apes have been trained to communicate using sign language.

Unfortunately, the survival of the primates is threatened by one of their own kind—humans. Although primates are protected by international laws, poachers kill them illegally. In addition, people are destroying many of the forests where primates live. Hopefully, the day will never come when monkeys, apes, and prosimians live only in zoos.

BUSH BABIES

The bush baby is a small, nocturnal primate with a very keen sense of smell. Its large eyes are ideal for seeing in the dark. Bush babies are exceptionally agile. If threatened by a snake or owl, they can make great leaps of escape. They also leap from tree to tree in search of fresh fruits and insects. They are called bush babies because they sometimes cry like a human baby. The loud cries warn other bush babies of snakes or birds in the area. One type of bush baby, the dwarf bush baby, is one of the smallest primates of all. A full-grown adult is no bigger than a squirrel.

RING-TAILED LEMURS

Ring-tailed lemurs are popular performers at zoos throughout the world. These well-known primates are often referred to as cat lemurs because they can purr like house cats. Wild ring-tailed lemurs live on the island of Madagascar, off the southeastern coast of Africa. The animal uses its long, ringed tail as a balancing tool. It helps the lemur jump from tree to tree. The lemur also uses its tail to scare off enemies. If threatened, the lemur soaks its tail with its scent, then waves it in the air. Most would-be attackers retreat after whiffing the foul smell.

RUFFED LEMURS

The ruffed lemur is the largest of all the lemurs. Like ringtails, ruffed lemurs live on the island of Madagascar. Except for some native hawks and eagles, the island is predator free. The ruffed lemur is too large to fall prey to an eagle attack, so it has no natural enemies. Like other lemurs, the ruffed lemur sleeps during the day and is active at night. During the night, the lemurs roam casually through the forest, eating fruits and vegetation. At daybreak, they bathe in the warm sunshine then build nests and sleep the day away.

COTTON-TOP MARMOSETS

The cotton-top marmoset is one of the smallest primates in the world. A full-grown adult is about the size of a small kitten. Marmosets live in the rain forests of northern South America. They usually stay in the treetops to avoid their enemies. Large birds, snakes, and wildcats like to snack on this tiny primate. Like most other animals, marmosets are always searching for something to eat. Their diet consists mainly of leaves, fruits, and insects. Despite its small size, a cotton-top marmoset raises quite a fury if another animal invades its feeding territory.

JAPANESE MACAQUES

Japanese macaques are often referred to as snow monkeys. These primates live in the mountains of northern Japan, where snow is abundant year-round. Japanese macaques have long, shaggy fur that helps keep them warm. They endure harsh winter storms by huddling close together. They also escape the cold by swimming in the natural hot springs that are found in the high mountains. The snow monkey's diet is limited to tree bark, buds, and twigs. During the night, they cling to the tops of pine trees to avoid lynx and coyotes—their only enemies.

SIAMANG MONKEYS

The siamang monkey is well known for its amazing calls. These monkeys sing to establish their territories. They also scream if they are frightened or in danger. Leopards, snakes, and large birds are all reasons for alarm to a siamang monkey. Siamangs also sing to celebrate the strong social bond of their troop. When the whole troop cries, it is the loudest sound in the jungle. The calls can carry over three miles. The large bulge in the siamang's throat is called a *throat sac*. The throat sac is about the size of a volleyball. It enhances the carrying quality of the monkey's call.

SPIDER MONKEYS

The spider monkey is one of the most active of all primates. It spends most of the day leaping through the treetops searching for ripe fruit to eat. As the monkey scurries about, its arms and tail bend at the joints. This gives the monkey the appearance of a crouching spider. The spider monkey's tail is strong and muscular. The monkey uses its tail to grasp tree limbs. The underside of the tail has a palmlike surface that helps the monkey keep a firm grip. Spider monkeys sometimes hang from their tails so they can use all four limbs to grab fruit.

RED UAKARIS

The brilliant red face of the uakari sets it apart from all other primates. The red face is brightest if the uakari spends a lot of time in the sun. These unusual primates live in the rain forests of South America. They live in large groups so they can warn one another of danger. Uakaris spend most of their time high in the forest, leaping from tree to tree. Like other monkeys, uakaris are vegetarians. They eat fruits, leaves, and seeds. Despite their fearsome appearance, uakaris are gentle and playful. In the 1800s, they were captured alive and kept as pets.

MANDRILLS

The mandrill is one of the most colorful monkeys in the world. The bright colors on the face of the male look much like war paint. Mandrills live in western Africa. They roam the forest in large groups, some consisting of up to 50 animals. Mandrills eat and sleep in the trees, but spend most of their time on the ground. They sometimes snack on insects, though they feed mainly on plants. Their large fangs are useful in cracking open hard nuts. Mandrills do not have many enemies. Their terrifying screams, large fangs, and fearsome looks scare away most attackers.

CHIMPANZEES

Apart from humans, chimpanzees are the most widely studied primates. Wild chimps are easy to find, follow, and observe. They are not at all afraid of humans. Chimpanzees sometimes entertain the scientists that come to study them. Chimps are very much like humans. They use simple tools for everyday tasks. To remove termites from a log, a chimpanzee uses a long stick coated with saliva. When the stick is pulled out, it is loaded with the chimp's favorite food. Chimpanzees are the only primates—besides humans—that eat meat.

MOUNTAIN GORILLAS

Mountain gorillas are the largest living apes. Adult males can weigh up to 450 pounds, though most are about the size of an average man. Mountain gorillas live in the high, evergreen forests of central Africa. Families of gorillas roam the forests, eating fruits, leaves, vegetables, and tree bark. Known for their strength, these ferocious-looking beasts are actually rather gentle and curious creatures. Sadly, mountain gorillas are nearly extinct, due mainly to the threat from humans. Hunters illegally kill mother gorillas in order to capture their young alive.

ORANGUTANS

In the native language of Indonesia, *orangutan* means "man of the forest." These gainly apes do indeed look and behave much like people. Apart from humans, orangutans are the smartest of all primates. In captivity, they can open childproof medicine bottles and have been taught sign language. Because of their intelligence, orangutans have starred in several motion pictures. Unfortunately, orangutans are not as happy as they look. To make room for our increasing population, humans are destroying the forests where wild orangutans live.

THE CHILD'S WORLD
NATUREBOOKS

Wildlife Library

Alligators	*Musk-oxen*
Arctic Foxes	*Octopuses*
Bald Eagles	*Owls*
Beavers	*Penguins*
Birds	*Polar Bears*
Black Widows	*Primates*
Camels	*Rattlesnakes*
Cheetahs	*Reptiles*
Coyotes	*Rhinoceroses*
Dogs	*Seals and Sea Lions*
Dolphins	*Sharks*
Elephants	*Snakes*
Fish	*Spiders*
Giraffes	*Tigers*
Insects	*Walruses*
Kangaroos	*Whales*
Lions	*Wildcats*
Mammals	*Wolves*
Monarchs	*Zebras*

Space Library

Earth	*The Moon*
Mars	*The Sun*

Adventure Library

Glacier National Park	*Yosemite*
The Grand Canyon	*Yellowstone National Park*